GRANDMA MOSES
A PAINTER OF RURAL AMERICA

About the WOMEN OF OUR TIME® Series

Today more than ever, children need role models whose lives can give them the inspiration and guidance to cope with a changing world. *WOMEN OF OUR TIME*, a series of biographies focusing on the lives of twentieth-century women, is the first such series designed specifically for the 7–11 age group. International in scope, these biographies cover a wide range of personalities—from historical figures to today's headliners—in such diverse fields as politics, the arts and sciences, athletics, and entertainment. Outstanding authors and illustrators present their subjects in a vividly anecdotal style, emphasizing the childhood and youth of each woman. More than a history lesson, the *WOMEN OF OUR TIME* books offer carefully documented life stories that will inform, entertain, and inspire the young people of our time.

"Another in an excellent series....Oneal's style is graceful and richly spiced with Grandma Moses' own pithy comments. Illustrated with reproductions that exemplify the succinct descriptions of Moses' paintings."
—*Bulletin of the Center for Children's Books*

GRANDMA MOSES

PAINTER OF RURAL AMERICA

BY ZIBBY ONEAL

Illustrations by Donna Ruff
Paintings by Grandma Moses

PUFFIN BOOKS

For Karen Alexander

PUFFIN BOOKS
Published by the Penguin Group
Penguin Books USA Inc.,
375 Hudson Street, New York, New York 10014, U.S.A.
Penguin Books Ltd, 27 Wrights Lane, London W8 5TZ, England
Penguin Books Australia Ltd, Ringwood, Victoria, Australia
Penguin Books Canada Ltd, 10 Alcorn Avenue, Toronto, Ontario, Canada M4V 3B2
Penguin Books (N.Z.) Ltd, 182–190 Wairau Road, Auckland 10, New Zealand

Penguin Books Ltd, Registered Offices: Harmondsworth, Middlesex, England

First published by Viking Penguin Inc., 1986
Published in Puffin Books 1987
9   10
Text copyright © Zibby Oneal, 1986
Illustrations copyright © Donna Ruff, 1986
All rights reserved
Set in Garamond #3
Women of Our Time ® is a registered trademark of Viking Penguin Inc.

Library of Congress catalog card number: 87–42800
ISBN 0-14-032220-5

Grateful acknowledgment is made for permission to reprint the following copyrighted
material: Quotes by Grandma Moses from *Grandma Moses, American Primitive,* Copyright
© 1946 (renewed 1974), Grandma Moses Properties Co., N.Y.; *My Life's History,*
Copyright © 1952 (renewed 1980, Grandma Moses Properties Co., N.Y.; and
Grandma Moses, The Artist Behind the Myth, Copyright © 1982, Grandma Moses
Properties Co., N.Y.
Grandma Moses illustrations copyright © 1986, Grandma Moses Properties Co., N.Y.
Cover painting, *In the Studio,* by Grandma Moses, courtesy Sidney Janis Gallery.
July Fourth painting, courtesy of the White House Collection.

CONTENTS

1

A Country Childhood

One morning at breakfast, Anna Mary's father told her that he'd dreamed about her the night before. Anna Mary Robertson was a little girl and she was curious about that dream. "Was it good or bad, Pa?"

"That depends on the future," her father replied. "Dreams cast their shadows before us."

Her father had dreamed that he was standing in a room where many people were gathered, all of them shouting and clapping their hands. What, he wondered, could be going on? Then, in the dream, he saw

Anna Mary coming toward him, walking on the shoulders of the people in the crowd. It seemed that the people were clapping for Anna Mary.

It was a strange dream. Anna Mary's mother thought it was all foolishness. But many years later, when Anna Mary Robertson had become an old woman known and loved the world around as the painter called Grandma Moses, she remembered her father's dream. Then she wondered whether dreams truly did cast their shadows into the future.

Anna Mary was born on a farm in eastern New York State, north of Albany, in the year 1860, just as the United States was entering the Civil War. She lived to be one hundred and one years old. When she was born, Lincoln was not yet President. There were only thirty-three states in the Union. In her lifetime, she saw the coming of electricity, cars, TV, and jet planes. Yet when she began to paint, most often she painted scenes from the childhood world she remembered.

Anna Mary was one of ten children. There were five boys and five girls, Anna Mary and three of her brothers being oldest. Later the other children came along. "We came in bunches," she said, "like radishes."

Anna Mary was named for her mother's sisters, but at home she was always called Sissy. It wasn't until she was six that she discovered she had another name, and that her brother Bubby had another one, too. It was the same way with birthdays. Anna Mary didn't know she *had* birthdays until she was seven and her mother explained to her what birthdays meant.

Anna Mary's parents were hardworking farm people, too busy to pay much attention to their children. But the children never doubted they were loved. As an old woman, Grandma Moses remembered her mother checking the children each night before she went to bed to make sure they were covered and warm.

Farm life in the second half of the last century was not easy. Almost everything a family needed, from clothes to candles, had to be made right on the farm. There was no electricity, no plumbing. Water was carried from a pump in the yard. There was no refrigeration. Food that could spoil was lowered in a basket into a well to keep cool.

Children had many jobs. They gathered eggs in the hen house, fed the chickens, and weeded the garden where the family's vegetables grew. When they were older, they learned to milk cows. They carried wood for the kitchen stove and hung wet laundry out to dry when they were tall enough to reach the line. There were plenty of chores for everyone on a farm.

When Anna Mary was old enough, she began to do her share of housework and to help her mother with the younger children. She didn't mind rocking the baby's cradle so much, but she preferred being outdoors with her brothers.

With them, she roamed the fields and surrounding woods, climbed trees in the orchard, and ate the fat black cherries that grew there. Together the children searched out wildflowers in the spring and set off firecrackers on the Fourth of July. At church picnics, they ate all the cake and lemonade they could hold. They went to county fairs. In summer they watched dark thunder clouds gather over Bald Mountain fifteen miles away, and ran for home before the storm, as the wind began to bend the treetops.

In winter they skated on the glassy black ice of frozen ponds. When the snow was deep, they got out their sleds and headed for the field above the orchard. Lester had the only real sled with iron runners. Horace had an upended wash bench. Arthur had a dustpan, and Anna Mary had a shovel. On these, they coasted the hill until their noses were numbed by the zero weather.

Sometimes there were sleigh rides. Their father would hitch the horses to their old red sleigh, and off they'd go, breaking a path through the snow to the main road. Then back again they came, around the

Out for Christmas Trees

barn, the children huddled under straw and blankets in the feathery falling snow.

In March, when the thaws began, Mr. Robertson tapped into the maple trees in the woods to collect sap from which to make maple syrup. It was the children's job to gather the sap buckets and carry them in damp, mittened hands to the large outdoor kettle where the sap was boiled all day over an open fire. Their reward was maple syrup on their pancakes, and a tea made of syrup and sweet fern fronds.

They chased the Thanksgiving turkey around the barnyard, intent on catching it for the holiday feast. At Christmastime, they trudged through deep snow into the silent woods, following their father, to cut a tall and fragrant tree.

Their days were spent in work and games, close to the outdoors and the changing seasons. Much, much later, when Anna Mary began to paint, her pictures recalled these happy days.

2

Outdoing the Boys

No matter what her brothers did, Anna Mary wanted to do it, too. In fact, she wanted to do it better. "It was a strife with me to outdo them," she said. "I wanted to be the big toad."

If Lester climbed partway up the roof of the house, Anna Mary climbed to the top. If he was allowed to walk the narrow edge above the rushing water of the millrace at their father's mill, Anna Mary wanted to follow right after. She tried her best to outdo the boys, but in one thing she failed: Lester could swim. Try as she might, Anna Mary could not. Her father often tried to teach her, holding her up in the water, but the moment he let her go, she sank.

All the same, Anna Mary was determined to do what the boys did. And so she was greatly surprised one day when she was almost nine years old to discover that there were times when she had to behave as ladies were expected to in those days.

On that day, there was company at dinner. To Anna Mary's shock, her brothers—even Arthur, who was younger than she—were permitted to sit at the table with the guests. Anna Mary was not. Ladies had to learn to wait until later, her mother told her. Anna Mary was not happy to wait. She began to cry. Then she began to yell.

Her father told her to stop the noise, but Anna Mary was too angry. She cried harder. He stood and took her by the arm. He led her outside to his carpentry shop and picked up a long wood shaving. This made Anna Mary madder still. She stamped her foot. She shouted, "If you strike me with that, I will never like you again!"

Her father looked down at her, and then he smiled. Though his beard was long, she could see the smile beneath, which seemed to say he knew how she felt. If her father had a favorite among his four oldest children, it was Anna Mary, the only girl, and she knew it. She knew, too, that the wood shaving he had

chosen to use as a whip would have crumbled had it touched her.

Grandma Moses remembered her father as a dreamer, and as a lover of beauty. He was himself something of a painter.

One winter, when he had been ill and was recovering from pneumonia, he decided to paint the walls in the house. He chose not to paint them a solid color, but to decorate them with pictures. He began in one corner of the room, painting a pretty spring scene he remembered. Mrs. Robertson thought the picture so

nice that she urged him to do more. And so, while the children tagged after, getting into his paint, he worked his way around the room, decorating the walls with pictures.

He often bought big sheets of white paper for a penny and gave them to the children to draw on, for he liked to see them drawing. The boys drew steam engines and animals, but Anna Mary was not satisfied with that. She thought she could do better. She wanted to do whole scenes. And she wanted to do them in color. Lacking paints, she used grape juice and crushed berries for color. Sometimes she used a stub of red or blue carpenter's chalk or the red dye that her father used to mark sheep—anything she could get her hands on that would make her pictures bright and cheerful.

Occasionally she painted on sticks of wood, or on pieces of slate or old windowpane. She liked doing pictures of the countryside, complete with brilliant sunsets. Her father encouraged her, saying the paintings weren't bad. But her brothers teased her because she called her paintings "lamb scapes."

Like her father, Anna Mary loved beautiful things. She loved color—the blue and purple wildflowers she found in the spring, the amber color of homemade soap, the pink apron with pockets her mother made her. She waited eagerly all one day for the red dress her father had promised to bring her from town, but when at last the dress arrived, she was disappointed. The red she'd hoped for was more nearly brown.

Though Anna Mary didn't much like sewing, she liked to knit lace in pretty patterns. She enjoyed making her own paper dolls, cutting them out and dressing them in flounced skirts made from the pink and green tissue paper her grandmother gave her. She painted the dolls' eyes with laundry bluing and colored their lips with grape juice. Every doll had a corset.

The Schoolhouse

Anna Mary liked to line her dolls up and admire them, but she had to be careful. Sometimes just as she'd gotten them all in line, one of the boys would appear and tear up the dolls to tease her.

Three months in the winter and three in summer the children went to school. The schoolhouse was a small, one-room building with a bell that hung above the door to call the children in. Children of all ages had classes together in the single room.

For Anna Mary, the best part of school was geography because the teacher let them draw maps. Anna Mary loved doing that. She drew a map of Colorado, putting in the mountains her own way. Range after range of them spread across the map, carefully drawn in pencil, looking like smocking on a party dress. Anna Mary's teacher liked her maps so well that he asked to be allowed to keep them.

Anna Mary's mother was a practical woman. To her way of thinking, maps and dolls and paintings were all very well, but it was more important that a girl learn the many skills a farm wife needed. There was cooking, for instance. A farm wife had to cook enormous meals to feed the hired men who came to help with the farming. And then there was laundry and sewing and making every sort of needed thing.

Anna Mary learned to make soap from grease and lye, and candles from beef tallow hardened in molds.

On wash day, she hauled out wooden tubs, a scrubbing board, and pails and learned to scrub and bleach and starch and hang out a bright, clean wash to dry. She learned to sew.

One evening, while they were doing supper dishes, her mother asked her how she'd like to have a new dress to wear. Of course, Anna Mary said she'd like one. And so as soon as they'd put the dishes away, Lester hitched the horses to the sleigh and drove Anna Mary and her mother into the village to buy the makings of a dress. He tied the horses to one of the hitching posts that lined the street, and they went into the drygoods store. Anna Mary felt a little afraid, for she'd never entered a store before.

The storekeeper brought out bolts of calico—one, a black-and-white print, the other a cinnamon brown. The black-and-white would wear better, her mother said, but Anna Mary chose the cinnamon brown.

The next day, after the chores were done, they spread the fabric on the table, and Anna Mary's mother showed her how to pin a pattern and cut out a dress. For a while, Anna Mary thought the job would be fun, but when the cloth was cut she saw she'd only begun. Now there was all the sewing to do. With needle and thread and thimble, she began to stitch the dress as her mother showed her. Her stitches had to be small and even, and it was a long and tiresome task. There was no sewing machine in the house. Every stitch of that dress had to be done by hand.

Though Anna Mary found housework tiresome and dull, she learned to do it, and soon the skills her mother taught her became very useful. At the age of twelve, she left home to earn her living. Like many young girls in those days, she decided to work as a hired girl for a family nearby.

She left in spite of her father's wishes. He had hoped that she would stay in school. But Anna Mary had other ideas. All her life long she had a streak of independence. She liked to make her own way.

3

The Bitter
and the Sweet

Anna Mary worked for fifteen years as a hired girl, first for one family and then for another. These were hard years. She worked long hours, cooking and cleaning and minding small children. There was little time for amusement. On Sundays she went to church and enjoyed the hymns and the sermons and the chance to see friends. She made some visits home. But mostly she worked.

During those years her brother Horace died, then her brother Arthur and finally her younger sister Miama. There were three funerals in six years. Remembering that time years later, Grandma Moses wrote simply, "We had to take the bitter with the sweet always."

And so it was. After these bitter days came a time of happiness.

In the fall of 1886, when she was 26, Anna Mary went to work for a family named James. She was to care for Mrs. James, who was ill, and to tend the small children. Working for the family at this time as a hired man was a young farmer named Thomas Moses.

Thomas liked Anna Mary's cooking. She liked his ways. He seemed a sensible and kind sort of man to her. She admired him. "Some women like a man because he is rich," she said, "but that kind of like is not lasting." Thomas was not rich, but she liked him. As time went on, they became engaged to marry.

Thomas was a tall, blue-eyed man who loved farming. He had always dreamed of having a farm of his own. When he and Anna Mary were engaged, they began to talk of going South to find a farm in a warmer climate.

They were married in a simple ceremony in the minister's parlor in Hoosick Falls, a town not far from the farm where Anna Mary was born. It was a late November afternoon, a year after they met.

Anna Mary wore a dark green dress and jacket, and a hat trimmed with a pink feather. She carried all the money she had in the world—thirty dollars—in the pocket of her jacket. This, together with a few books and some feather mattresses and pillows, was her dowry. Thomas carried the few hundred dollars he had saved in a red cloth bag tucked inside his undershirt.

After the ceremony, there was a wedding supper planned complete with wedding cake, but the bride and groom could not stay to enjoy it. They were heading South, and they had to hurry to catch a six o'clock train that would take them on the first leg of their journey.

They had said goodbye to Anna Mary's family several days before, not knowing when they would see them next. Travel wasn't easy then, and distances seemed greater. Anna Mary's father was sorry to see her go, thinking of his brothers and sisters whom he rarely saw who lived only as far away as Buffalo. Anna Mary was going much farther.

Now they bid Thomas's family goodbye and hurried for their train. That evening, they reached Albany. On the next day, they took a train to New York City, then another on to Washington, and so on, taking one train and then another, going South.

At last, after four days' traveling, they came to Staunton, Virginia, in the heart of the Shenandoah Valley. It was mid-November and cold up North, but here in Virginia there were flowers.

They had meant to go farther—on to North Carolina where Thomas had the promise of work—but there were people in Staunton who urged them to stay. There was a farm for rent, complete with furniture and kitchenware, some livestock and a cat. The Virginians were kind and generous folk. As things turned out, they stayed.

At first Anna Mary was not entirely comfortable in the South. She vowed never to have a Southern accent, and some of the words the Southerners used confused her. "Bucket" and "tote," for instance. These were words she swore she'd never use when she meant "pail" and "carry." Nor would she say "poke" when she meant "paper bag." Yet little by little, she fell into doing this.

The Civil War had ended twenty-two years before Thomas and Anna Mary came South. The slaves had long been free, but in Virginia there were many blacks who had been slaves as children. From time to time, some of these freed slaves came to work on the farm, helping Thomas with the farming and, later, helping Anna Mary with the children. To Anna Mary, a Yankee, these people were like part of the family, but just as she had begun to accept Southern phrases, so she came to accept Southern ways. At that time in Virginia, blacks and whites never ate together at the same table. So when Anna Mary set tables for the farm workers, she set them separately for blacks and whites, though the custom seemed strange and pointless to her.

From the beginning, Anna Mary had believed that she and Thomas were a team. She was determined to do her share, as much as he did. She had no use for women who sat around, waiting for someone "to throw sugar at them." She never had. And so to help out, she took her money and bought a cow. And that was the beginning of the butter business.

One spring day, when she had extra butter left from her churning—more than they could use themselves—she urged Thomas to take it into town and exchange it for groceries. She wrapped the butter in burdock leaves to keep it cool, tucked it into a milk pail, and off it went. The grocer tasted it and asked for more. He called it "Yankee butter" and he offered her twenty cents a pound. By fall Anna Mary had sold enough butter to pay for two cows.

The butter business grew and grew. Soon Thomas and Anna Mary moved to a large dairy farm a little farther down the river. Anna Mary was churning butter three times a day. While she churned, she looked off over the valley to where, far in the distance, the trains came through, their smoke rolling up pale and hazy against the Blue Ridge Mountains. She often wished that she could paint that scene—the white smoke against the misty blue.

But there was no time for painting in those days. In December, a little girl was born whom they named Winona. Soon, while Anna Mary churned, the baby was playing on the floor beside her, pulling on the cats' tails.

Then came Loyd and Forrest, and finally there were ten babies in all, though only five—Loyd and Forrest, Winona, Hugh, and Anna—lived to grow up. As an old woman, Grandma Moses remembered wistfully the five little graves she had left behind in the Shenandoah Valley.

Like her mother before her, Anna Mary was too busy to fuss much over her children. In summer, she put them in sun bonnets so they wouldn't burn and tied the children so they wouldn't fall into the river. Later, when they were too old to be tied and had begun to play on the narrow bridge that spanned the water, she decided not to worry. Thomas told her it was no use.

She didn't scold her children much. She rarely lost her temper. When she was angry, she had learned to keep quiet and to say to herself, "Ishkabibble." Doing that calmed her down, she thought, so that she didn't do or say something she'd regret.

Sometimes, if she had to, she whipped the children with switches that she made them cut from a lilac bush. She didn't whip hard. She figured that cutting the switches was half the punishment.

The children grew and soon they were old enough for school. It was then that Anna Mary began her potato chip business. It started in the way the butter business had, with Anna Mary trying to help out and do her share.

She began in a small way, slicing up a few pounds of potatoes, frying them crisp, and sending them to the grocer to trade for other things she needed. Potato chips were a novelty in those days, and soon she was sending them as far away as Charlottesville and White Sulphur Springs and making a good profit. That made her proud. It was like climbing to the top of the house in her childhood, she thought, a large accomplishment. Just as then, she still wanted to be "the big toad." But now, while Anna Mary grew fonder and fonder of the Shenandoah Valley, Thomas grew homesick for the North. He wanted to go back. And so, after almost twenty years of living in Virginia, they began to pack up for the return.

They rented a railroad car and filled it with their household goods. They added their chickens and a cow, several bushels of apples, a butchered hog, and finally their little dog, Brownie. Thomas, Loyd, and Forrest rode along in the railroad car to look after the animals. Anna Mary and the other children took another train.

They came to a farm in Eagle Bridge, New York, where they settled down, not far from Anna Mary's

Home in the Springtime

birthplace. The children's Yankee cousins called them "rebels." Anna Mary thought longingly of Virginia, where the train smoke rolled up white against the mountains.

They called the farm in Eagle Bridge, Mt. Nebo. The children went to school in the same one-room schoolhouse their mother had. Then they grew up and went away to school. And then they married and went away for good. Some stayed close by. Some went farther. And for the first time in many years, the house was not full of children.

Anna Mary began to paint a little. At first, the paintings were almost accidents. Once, when she was wallpapering her parlor, she ran short of paper to cover the fireboard that served as a screen before the fireplace. Well, why not paint it instead? That seemed like a good idea.

She pasted a piece of paper over the board, then painted it a solid color. Now, like her father before her, she decided to paint a scene. She added two large trees and a lake—a bright yellow lake as if seen in sunlight. In the foreground she added bushes, painting the entire scene with a brush she'd used to paint the floor. People admired the fireboard. "That," she said, "was my first large picture."

Another time, Thomas salvaged the window from an old caboose. Anna Mary seized on this and painted

the window's glass on both sides, covering it with pictures. She made little paintings sometimes to give away as presents, but she didn't take her painting very seriously.

Neither did Thomas. He didn't pay it much mind until one evening when he happened to see a picture that took his fancy. Who'd painted it? he wanted to know. Anna Mary had, of course. It was a gift she'd made—a little boy in blue standing beside a fence. Thomas liked it.

"Oh, that isn't much," Anna Mary said.

"No, that's real good," said Thomas.

And after that, often when Anna Mary began to paint, he stood and watched her. They were an old couple now, forty years married.

Thomas died quietly on a snowy January evening in 1927. Anna Mary was close by. Ever after, she remembered that when they were courting he had said that he would never leave her. She believed that somehow he never had.

Often when she was painting, she thought of him. "It was just as though he had something to do about this painting business," she wrote. "I wonder if he is watching over me."

4

Paintings in a Drugstore Window

Now Anna Mary was more than seventy. She lived with her youngest son, Hugh, and his wife, Dorothy. Sometimes she went to visit her other children and the grandchildren growing up nearby.

On one such visit, her daughter, Anna, described to her mother a picture she'd seen and liked. It was made of bright-colored worsted yarn embroidered on cloth. A whole little picture, it was, made of yarn! Anna thought her mother could do one as pretty, maybe even a better one. Anna Mary decided to try. She had time now for what she called "fancy work."

The first picture was a great success. Everyone admired what Grandma had done, and so she did another. And then another. She gave them away as gifts.

These pictures are little landscapes—snowy scenes or summer scenes with houses and barns, sometimes a covered bridge, often flowers. The yarns are bright and many shaded for, just as she had as a little girl, Grandma Moses loved color.

She made a number of these worsted pictures before her hands became too lame. Rheumatism made it hard for her to hold a needle, and her sister, Celestia, suggested that perhaps she ought to try painting instead. It would be faster and easier for her than embroidery. Grandma Moses agreed. And so she began to paint again. One of the first pictures was done in housepaint on an old piece of canvas that had been used to mend the cover on the threshing machine.

When Grandma had finished quite a few paintings, Hugh and Dorothy decided to gather some of them together and take them, with a few of the worsted pictures, down to the town of Hoosick Falls. There, in the W. D. Thomas Pharmacy, was a women's exchange where local women could display and sell things they'd made. Mrs. Thomas was pleased to have Grandma Moses's paintings. She put several in the drugstore window.

At about the same time, Grandma Moses sent an

Country Fair

assortment of her canned fruit and jam to the nearby Cambridge Fair. She also sent along a few of her paintings. She won prizes for her fruit and jam, but no one bought a picture. Nor was anyone buying the pictures in the drugstore window until one day when something important happened.

On that day, a man from New York City named Louis J. Caldor was passing through Hoosick Falls. He happened to glance in the drugstore window, and he liked the paintings he saw there. He went into the store to ask about them. When he came out, he had the paintings under his arm and Grandma Moses's address in his pocket. He wanted to buy more.

When Grandma Moses heard this, she was astonished. He'd bought those pictures and he wanted more! How many more did he want? she wondered. Someone had told him that there might be as many more as ten.

Grandma Moses spent a sleepless night. She was trying to remember where other pictures might be. She didn't think there *were* ten more pictures. Maybe, together with her worsted pictures, there were almost enough. But ten? Toward morning, she thought of a solution. There was a painting—quite a large one— she remembered. If she could find a couple of frames in the morning, she could saw the picture in half and have two.

She did just that. When Mr. Caldor arrived, she had ten pictures to show him.

Louis Caldor was a civil engineer and he was an art collector. He liked Grandma Moses. He liked her work. And he set out to help her in every way he could. He sent her paints from New York which were much better than the ones she'd been using. He wrote her letters of encouragement. He took her pictures from one art gallery to another, trying to interest people in her work.

He spent many months going from gallery to gallery. Again and again, he was turned down. Nobody seemed to care enough about Grandma Moses's paintings to be willing to exhibit them in New York. But Louis Caldor was not a man to give up easily. He kept trying.

At last he heard of a show that was being organized at The Museum of Modern Art in New York. It was to be called "Contemporary Unknown American Painters." Mr. Caldor went to see the man who was organizing the show.

This man, Sidney Janis, was someone who knew a great deal about painting. He looked at the pictures Mr. Caldor had brought and chose three of them.

Louis Caldor was overjoyed. He wrote to Grandma Moses that he had kept his promise to her. He had persisted until at last someone else saw how good her paintings were. Now the pictures were to be shown in a great museum.

The paintings appeared in the show that fall, but after that not much changed. When the exhibit closed, the paintings were returned to Mr. Caldor. He set out again in search of others who would share his enthusiasm.

It was in this way that the paintings came finally to a man who was to have great and lasting importance in Grandma Moses's life. He was the man who, in time, would help to make her work known the world over. His name was Otto Kallir.

Otto Kallir was an art dealer who had come to the United States from Austria and had opened a gallery in New York City called the Galerie St. Etienne. He was very much interested in American folk art, works by artists who had taught themselves to paint. Mr. Caldor, when he learned this, went at once to see Otto Kallir with his collection of Grandma Moses's paintings.

Mr. Kallir was interested in what he saw. He liked especially a painting of a sugaring-off—a landscape in which figures bustled about performing the many tasks required in the making of maple syrup. Here was the snowy countryside, the kettle boiling on an open fire, small figures bringing in the buckets of sap, everyone working. Kallir thought that the little figures were

Sugaring Off

clumsy, but the landscape impressed him a great deal. He offered to give Grandma Moses a show in his gallery.

The exhibit was called "What a Farmwife Painted." It opened in the fall of 1940, the year Grandma Moses was eighty. Mr. Kallir invited her to come to New York City for the opening. Grandma Moses said no. There wasn't much point to that. As she said, she *had*, after all, seen the paintings before!

5

"The White-Haired Girl of the U.S.A."

Grandma Moses is called a primitive painter or folk artist, meaning that she never had lessons or formal training in painting. What she knew about painting, she taught herself.

There have been many such self-taught painters in America, though few as famous as Grandma Moses became. Until well into the nineteenth century, there were no art schools in the United States of the sort found in Europe. Artists who could not travel to Europe simply had to learn what they could from others, or from the study of prints and engravings that came their way.

Grandma Moses learned in this way, too. She studied the pictures on greeting cards and calendars, the illustrations that appealed to her in magazines and newspapers. She especially liked lithographs of New England farm scenes that were published by Currier and Ives. These recalled her own childhood—sledding and skating, sugaring and sleigh-riding, and the many farm tasks she remembered well. They were the subjects she painted most often. She liked, she said, to paint "old-timey" things.

For some time, these illustrations were her models and she copied them closely. Sometimes she cut figures from the illustrations and pasted them right onto her own work. Other times she merely used the cutouts to help her to compose a scene, arranging them here and there on her picture, pinning them down with sewing needles until she had a composition she liked.

Then one day, she happened to glimpse the shiny hubcap of a car in her yard. In it she saw a tiny scene reflected—the house and trees and figures around her—all mirrored there in a perfect little picture. This was a far better picture than any she'd been copying, she thought, and it was a scene she could see through her own window. By standing at the window and moving a little to the right or left, she could frame the scene in a number of ways. This changed her ideas about painting.

From this time on, her inspiration came from the landscape around her, though she continued to use her little cutouts as models for the figures in the paintings. She was never so comfortable with figures as she was with the countryside. In all her work, the figures remain clumsy in comparison to the soft blue hills and the yellow or green or snowy fields that are their setting.

Grandma Moses worked in her bedroom at a tip-up table that had belonged to an ancestor. Mostly she painted on Masonite board because it lasted. Before she began to paint, she found frames, then sawed the board up to fit them. A picture without a frame was like a woman without a dress, she thought. All her pictures had frames.

Next she took a big house-painter's brush and gave the board a few coats of white paint. When this dried, she was ready to pencil in a scene. Then she painted.

To create the shades she wanted, Grandma Moses mixed her paints in the lids of preserve jars. Sometimes she didn't mix them at all, but squeezed paint from the tube directly onto the brush, like toothpaste. For small details like eyes and mouths, she abandoned a brush altogether and used a pin or a matchstick. She liked to sprinkle her snow scenes with "glitter," even though experts tried to tell her that no true painter would do that. Well, why not? she wanted to know.

Halloween

Anyone looking at snow on a sunny day could see right away that it glittered.

Like many painters, Grandma Moses usually worked on several paintings at once. Her reasons were practical. "I squeeze out a spot of green on my palette, then I paint everything that's going to be green in the pictures I'm working on." She added, "Saves lots of paint to work this way. Don't dry up on you."

The more she painted, the surer she became in handling her materials. She liked to say that the better brushes and paints that were sent from New York City were responsible for her improvement, but in fact the more she painted the more she learned. She was teaching herself more about painting all the time.

"I never know how I'm going to paint until I start in," she wrote. She started in every day, getting up at six o'clock and painting for five or six hours.

Shortly before the show closed at the Galerie St. Etienne, Gimbels, a large department store in New York City, asked to have the pictures for an exhibit during their Thanksgiving festivities. They advertised the event enthusiastically. Grandma Moses's age was made much of. "She's the white-haired girl of the U.S.A. who turned from her strawberry patch to painting the American scene at the wonderful age of eighty," the ad read.

Of course, Grandma Moses was invited to attend. This time she accepted.

She arrived bringing homemade bread and jam. She came ready to talk about these, not her painting, and was surprised to see the number of people gathered to greet her.

She entered the hall where the paintings were hung. Somebody pinned a microphone to her dress. "It felt just like a black bug," she said. Sitting on the platform, she was astonished to discover that this black bug was carrying everything she said to the 400 people in the room.

She was an instant success. Everyone was charmed by this little old lady in her black dress and stockings and her prim straw hat, sitting there among jars of homemade preserves.

Grandma Moses had her own way of saying things, and this delighted people, too. Once, when asked about the colors she chose, she replied, "There's no gettin' away from it, certain colors fascinate me. Take this bluish green edgin' my apron. I could almost eat that color, I like it so well."

At first it was her personality and her age as much as her art that attracted attention. But even as early as the Gimbels show there were others besides Louis Caldor and Otto Kallir who were looking seriously at her work.

As far as Grandma Moses was concerned, New York City was too much hustle-bustle. She was used to the quiet of Eagle Bridge. In the city, she was forever shaking hands and rushing from one place to another. She appreciated the bother people had gone to, but she was ready to go home.

All the attention didn't impress her much. When an interviewer asked how she felt about her sudden fame, she replied, "Well, people tell me they're proud to be seen on the street with me. But I just say, 'Well, why weren't you proud to be seen with me before?'"

6

Suddenly Famous

Back home in Eagle Bridge, Grandma Moses settled down quietly. But in the world beyond Eagle Bridge, her reputation began to grow like a snowball.

In 1941 one of her paintings, *The Old Oaken Bucket,* won the New York State Prize for painting. A year later, there was an exhibition of her work at the American British Art Center in New York City. Soon she was being invited to enter her paintings in exhibits all over New York State.

And now the orders began coming in. All at once everyone wanted an original Grandma Moses, or so it seemed. Callers appeared at the farm. Letters arrived. More and more people saw Grandma Moses's work and wanted paintings of their own.

In fact, they wanted paintings *exactly* like one or another they'd seen. "Paint me another *Oaken Bucket,*" a letter might say, or "Could you paint another sugaring-off picture?" Sometimes these orders included a description of what was wanted, or even a sketch to jog Grandma's memory.

Grandma tried to oblige. As she saw it, these people were her customers, just like those who had bought her butter and potato chips, and if they wanted another *Old Oaken Bucket,* then she aimed to please them. Yet she never took the easy way and copied herself exactly. Though the subject might be the same, each painting was a little different.

Together with orders came advice from the customers. They told her to paint larger pictures. They wanted her to hurry up, or to take her time. Grandma mostly ignored the advice.

She didn't like to hurry with a painting. She liked to take her time and work at a picture until it suited her. Then she liked to let it "settle" for a while. She didn't intend to hurry up.

She *did* begin painting a few larger pictures. Ordinarily her paintings were small enough to fit comfortably on her tip-up table. With larger pictures she

was stuck for someplace to paint. She solved the problem by using her bed as an easel, laying the board or canvas flat on the mattress and walking around the bed to reach all sides. It was hard work. Since the paintings were bigger, she charged more.

It was Grandma Moses's custom to set her prices according to the size of the picture, and she didn't like to charge much. "I tell folks if they have $10 to spend for a picture, they'd be better to put it in chickens. They multiply."

The prices being paid for her paintings in New York baffled her. As she saw it, she painted a picture, set a price, and that was that. When Otto Kallir began to sell her paintings for a great deal more than she asked, and to send her checks, she didn't like it. Sometimes she sent the checks back.

It was the same with her growing fame. She didn't want it. In particular, she minded being called a primitive painter. A neighbor had asked if that meant she couldn't read and write.

Nevertheless, her fame grew. In 1944, Otto Kallir gave two more exhibits of her work at his gallery. Beginning the same year, collections of her paintings began to be shown in many cities in the United States. A few years later there were shows in Europe.

Everyone wanted to interview Grandma Moses. She spoke on the radio. Magazines and newspapers loved to quote her. Again and again she was asked about her work, and over and over she insisted that anyone could paint. To one interviewer she said, "Could you sweep this floor? You could. But you'd have to get about doing it. That's how it is with paintin'."

In the next few years, Grandma Moses's work began to be reproduced in a number of forms: in large prints, on greeting cards, on plates and printed fabric. A book edited by Otto Kallir, called *Grandma Moses, American Primitive,* was published containing reproductions of forty of her paintings. Grandma Moses was fast becoming a household name.

For many people, her life was an inspiration. It was wonderful to think that a woman who had had one career as mother and wife and hard-working farm woman should begin another in her eighties with equal energy and optimism.

For others, it was wonderful to see in the peaceful country scenes she painted an America that they wanted to believe in. In the late 1940s, the United States was recovering from a great world war. The atomic bomb cast a long, frightening shadow across the countries of the world. Life seemed dangerous and uncertain in the aftermath of the Holocaust and Hiroshima, and human beings seemed frighteningly capable of evil. In Grandma Moses's paintings they saw something else.

It may be that people looking at her paintings in the 1940s were encouraged to remember that life can be as good as it can be bad. The paintings speak of the beauty of the countryside in storm and snow and sunshine, and of the quiet pleasures of work and play and family life. To a world recovering from war, Grandma Moses's paintings were a reminder of what the world *could* be.

In 1949 The Women's National Press Club awarded Grandma Moses a prize for "Outstanding Accomplishment in Art."

Grandma Moses was 88 that spring. As had so often been true in her life, there was bitter mixed with the sweet that year. In February her son Hugh had died suddenly. But in May she went to Washington, D.C., to receive the award from Harry Truman, the President of the United States.

On the day following the award ceremony, Grandma Moses had tea at Blair House with the President. As they sat chatting, a thunderstorm blew up. Lightning flickered outside the room's tall windows. The President assured Grandma Moses that the building had plenty of lightning rods, and this amused her. She supposed the President thought she was afraid!

She liked Mr. Truman. He was a country boy, she said, like one of her own. She thought he liked cows.

When the storm had passed, she asked him to play

the piano for, as everyone knew then, the President played. At first he was reluctant, offering to turn on the radio instead. But Grandma somehow had her way, and in the end the President sat down and played her a minuet. Every year after that, he sent her a birthday card.

Of course, there were reporters who wanted to interview Grandma Moses. There always were. By now she was growing used to them. They didn't bother her. In fact, they made her think of chickens flocking around when you came to the door to feed them. Did she and the President talk politics? one reporter wanted to know. "No," said Grandma, "we talked ploughin'."

What a crowd there was in Eagle Bridge to welcome Grandma Moses home! The town's one street was jammed with cars. Schoolchildren were on hand to present a bouquet. The Hoosick Falls High School Band played and escorted Grandma home. Such a celebration had rarely been seen in Eagle Bridge, but then, what other citizen of Eagle Bridge had been presented with an award by the President of the United States?

Grandma Moses had become very famous indeed.

7

"After You Get to Be About So Old"

A painting called *July Fourth* hangs in the White House. Like all Grandma Moses's work, it celebrates the spirit of rural America. It seems appropriate that Otto Kallir should have presented this painting of the country's birthday to President and Mrs. Truman after Grandma Moses's visit.

In the years that followed her trip to Washington, Grandma Moses was busy. Besides painting every day, she starred in a documentary film made of her life in Eagle Bridge. She wrote her autobiography, called *My Life's History*. She moved from the old family farm-

July Fourth

house to a smaller, more convenient one across the road. And in 1955, she went on television.

Edward R. Murrow, a well-known television personality, wrote to Grandma Moses asking to interview her for his program, *See It Now*. He also arranged to film Grandma painting, working as she always did, at home on her tip-up table.

The filming took place in June in the middle of a heat wave. Camera crews set up their lights and equipment in Grandma Moses's living room. The tip-up table was brought from her bedroom. Grandma's supplies were arranged around her. While the cameras recorded it, Grandma Moses set to work.

She had chosen to do a sugaring-off scene. As usual, she coated her board with white paint first, using her big house-painter's brush. Then she lightly penciled in the horizon and began to paint the sky. It would be an overcast winter sky, she said. Otherwise she'd have used a light blue.

From time to time, she paused and closed her eyes, as if considering what would come next. Then quickly she sketched in a tree or a bit of a figure and continued painting.

The filming went on for several days. The heat was made worse by the hot lights. Only Grandma Moses seemed to remain cool and calm. She moved from one section of the picture to another, adding a building here, a figure there. When she finished, she sprinkled the snow with "glitter."

The interview with Mr. Murrow began with a few questions, and in no time Grandma Moses was asking questions herself. Could he paint? She handed him a sheet of paper and told him to draw something. Mr. Murrow sketched a tree. Then he brought up another question. What did she plan to do in the next twenty years? he asked. Grandma Moses calmly raised her hand toward heaven. "I am going up yonder," she said. "Naturally—naturally I should. After you get to be about so old you can't expect to go on much farther."

But on she went. When she was ninety-six, Grandma Moses was asked to paint a picture for the new President, Dwight Eisenhower. His cabinet members wanted a painting of his farm in Gettysburg to mark the third anniversary of his inauguration.

Grandma admired the President. He was a painter himself, and had sent her a signed reproduction of one of his own paintings. She agreed to try doing a picture of his farm.

Then she was bewildered. She had never seen the farm, and she almost never painted scenes she did not know from firsthand experience. But from the photographs she was sent she created two pictures—the farm seen from two perspectives—and let the President's cabinet make the choice.

President Eisenhower was delighted. Grandma Moses had changed things around a bit, and he liked this. His golf green had grown in the picture to twice its size, and his cattle had changed breed. No matter. He would have liked such a golf green, he said.

Grandma Moses's one hundredth birthday was proclaimed Grandma Moses Day in New York State. Bags of birthday cards began arriving at the Eagle Bridge post office. As the day approached, there were

telegrams and dozens of gifts, which were stored on Grandma's sun porch among her plants and flowers.

Grandma Moses took all this in stride. A tiny old woman, dressed in her best, white hair in a knot on top of her head, a black ribbon at her throat, she received her visitors cheerfully. On her ninetieth birthday, someone had asked how she planned to spend her hundredth. "I have invited a few of my friends over for a dance then," she said. Now, on her hundredth, she danced a brief jig.

Grandma Moses painted twenty-six more pictures after her hundredth birthday. She did illustrations for a new edition of *'Twas the Night Before Christmas*, now sometimes having to steady one hand with the other. She didn't live to see this book published.

Gradually her strength was beginning to fail, but her family could not persuade her to rest. She longed to keep painting. One day she knelt down to pick up a tube of white paint. When she tried to get up, she couldn't.

In July, when Grandma was nearly 101, she went into a nursing home in Hoosick Falls where she could rest and be taken care of. She hated it. They wouldn't let her paint. As soon as she got home, she'd start again, she promised. But they didn't let her go.

One day, thoroughly put out, she hid the doctor's stethoscope. "It's a forfeit," she said. "You take me back to Eagle Bridge and you'll get back your stethoscope."

She never went back. On an early afternoon in December 1961, Grandma Moses died, leaving behind eleven grandchildren, thirty-one great-grandchildren, and a whole world of admirers. She had just worn out, her doctor said. It was as if her painting had kept her going and, without it, she had finally grown old.

Her paintings have not grown old. There are the memories of a busy country life in all the bright colors Grandma Moses loved. There are the misty blue hills of her childhood, the sleighs rushing over glittering snow. There are the ploughings and hayings, sugarings and celebrations remembered over a lifetime. There the seasons change, one following another, and the clouds drift over the curves of the earth.

"If I didn't start painting, I would have raised chickens," Grandma Moses wrote. We are lucky that she decided to paint.

Before I began to write this book about Grandma Moses, I looked and looked at her paintings. They hang in many museums. At the museum in Bennington, Vermont, I saw both her paintings and her schoolhouse, which now stands on the museum grounds. It is filled with objects she used in her daily life, including her tip-up table. From there it was a short drive to Eagle Bridge, New York, where I saw the farmhouse in which Grandma lived and painted, surrounded by the hills and fields she loved.

I read about her life as told in her own words and in books by Otto Kallir and Jane Kallir, both of which contain many reproductions of her work. I read articles written about Grandma during her lifetime, but, most important, I looked at her art.

If I were not a writer, I'd like to be a painter. In my novels, my characters sometimes are. I'm not sure I agree with Grandma that anyone can paint. But I'm certain that anyone can learn, by looking, to share the artist's eye.

To share Grandma Moses's eye is to see a world that is happy and hopeful. It's a world full of the pleasures of being alive.   Z.O.